MW00899026

Daily Cash Flow Log Book

NAME: ____________________

EMAIL: ____________________

PHONE: ____________________

ADDRESS: ____________________

Daily Cash Flow Log Book

Date: From To

Prey. Balance:

Date	Description	Cash in	Cash out	Balance
Total				

Date:

Signed:

Daily Cash Flow Log Book

Date: From To

Prev. Balance:

Date	Description	Cash in	Cash out	Balance
Total				

Date:

Signed:

Daily Cash Flow Log Book

Date: From To

Prey. Balance:

Date	Description	Cash in	Cash out	Balance
Total				

Date:

Signed:

Daily Cash Flow Log Book

Date: From To

Prev. Balance:

Date	Description	Cash in	Cash out	Balance
Total				

Date:

Signed:

DAILY CASH FLOW LOG BOOK

DATE: FROM　　　TO

PREV. BALANCE:

DATE	DESCRIPTION	CASH IN	CASH OUT	BALANCE
TOTAL				

DATE:

SIGNED:

Daily Cash Flow Log Book

Date: From To

Prey. Balance:

Date	Description	Cash in	Cash out	Balance
	Total			

Date:

Signed:

Daily Cash Flow Log Book

Date: From To

Prey. Balance:

Date	Description	Cash in	Cash out	Balance
Total				

Date:

Signed:

Daily Cash Flow Log Book

Date: From To

Prev. Balance:

Date	Description	Cash in	Cash out	Balance
Total				

Date:

Signed:

Daily Cash Flow Log Book

Date: From To

Prev. Balance:

Date	Description	Cash in	Cash out	Balance
Total				

Date:

Signed:

Daily Cash Flow Log Book

Date: From To

Prev. Balance:

Date	Description	Cash in	Cash out	Balance
Total				

Date:

Signed:

DAILY CASH FLOW LOG BOOK

DATE: FROM TO

PREV. BALANCE:

DATE	DESCRIPTION	CASH IN	CASH OUT	BALANCE
TOTAL				

DATE:

SIGNED:

Daily Cash Flow Log Book

Date: From To

Prev. Balance:

Date	Description	Cash in	Cash out	Balance
Total				

Date:

Signed:

Daily Cash Flow Log Book

Date: From To

Prev. Balance:

Date	Description	Cash in	Cash out	Balance
Total				

Date:

Signed:

DAILY CASH FLOW LOG BOOK

DATE: FROM TO

PREV. BALANCE:

DATE	DESCRIPTION	CASH IN	CASH OUT	BALANCE
	TOTAL			

DATE:

SIGNED:

Daily Cash Flow Log Book

Date: From To

Prey. Balance:

Date	Description	Cash in	Cash out	Balance
Total				

Date:

Signed:

Daily Cash Flow Log Book

Date: From To

Prey. Balance:

Date	Description	Cash in	Cash out	Balance
Total				

Date:

Signed:

Daily Cash Flow Log Book

Date: From To

Prev. Balance:

Date	Description	Cash in	Cash out	Balance
Total				

Date:

Signed:

Daily Cash Flow Log Book

Date: From To

Prey. Balance:

Date	Description	Cash in	Cash out	Balance
Total				

Date:

Signed:

Daily Cash Flow Log Book

Date: From To

Prev. Balance:

Date	Description	Cash in	Cash out	Balance
Total				

Date:

Signed:

Daily Cash Flow Log Book

Date: From To

Prey. Balance:

Date	Description	Cash in	Cash out	Balance
Total				

Date:

Signed:

Daily Cash Flow Log Book

Date: From To

Prey. Balance:

Date	Description	Cash in	Cash out	Balance
Total				

Date:

Signed:

Daily Cash Flow Log Book

Date: From To

Prev. Balance:

Date	Description	Cash in	Cash out	Balance
Total				

Date:

Signed:

Daily Cash Flow Log Book

Date: From To

Prev. Balance:

Date	Description	Cash in	Cash out	Balance
Total				

Date:

Signed:

Daily Cash Flow Log Book

Date: From To

Prey. Balance:

Date	Description	Cash in	Cash out	Balance
Total				

Date:

Signed:

Daily Cash Flow Log Book

Date: From To

Prev. Balance:

Date	Description	Cash in	Cash out	Balance
Total				

Date:

Signed:

Daily Cash Flow Log Book

Date: From To

Prey. Balance:

Date	Description	Cash in	Cash out	Balance
Total				

Date:

Signed:

Daily Cash Flow Log Book

Date: From To

Prev. Balance:

Date	Description	Cash in	Cash out	Balance
Total				

Date:

Signed:

Daily Cash Flow Log Book

Date: From To

Prev. Balance:

Date	Description	Cash in	Cash out	Balance
Total				

Date:

Signed:

Daily Cash Flow Log Book

Date: From To

Prev. Balance:

Date	Description	Cash in	Cash out	Balance
Total				

Date:

Signed:

Daily Cash Flow Log Book

Date: From To

Prev. Balance:

Date	Description	Cash in	Cash out	Balance
Total				

Date:

Signed:

Daily Cash Flow Log Book

Date: From To

Prey. Balance:

Date	Description	Cash in	Cash out	Balance
Total				

Date:

Signed:

Daily Cash Flow Log Book

Date: From To

Prey. Balance:

Date	Description	Cash In	Cash Out	Balance
Total				

Date:

Signed:

Daily Cash Flow Log Book

Date: From To

Prey. Balance:

Date	Description	Cash in	Cash out	Balance
Total				

Date:

Signed:

Daily Cash Flow Log Book

Date: From To

Prev. Balance:

Date	Description	Cash in	Cash out	Balance
Total				

Date:

Signed:

Daily Cash Flow Log Book

Date: From To

Prey. Balance:

Date	Description	Cash in	Cash out	Balance
Total				

Date:

Signed:

DAILY CASH FLOW LOG BOOK

DATE: FROM TO

PREY. BALANCE:

DATE	DESCRIPTION	CASH IN	CASH OUT	BALANCE
TOTAL				

DATE:

SIGNED:

Daily Cash Flow Log Book

Date: From To

Prev. Balance:

Date	Description	Cash in	Cash out	Balance
Total				

Date:

Signed:

Daily Cash Flow Log Book

Date: From To

Prev. Balance:

Date	Description	Cash in	Cash out	Balance
Total				

Date:

Signed:

DAILY CASH FLOW LOG BOOK

DATE: FROM TO

PREY. BALANCE:

DATE	DESCRIPTION	CASH IN	CASH OUT	BALANCE
TOTAL				

DATE:

SIGNED:

Daily Cash Flow Log Book

Date: From To

Prev. Balance:

Date	Description	Cash In	Cash Out	Balance
Total				

Date:

Signed:

Daily Cash Flow Log Book

Date: From To

Prev. Balance:

Date	Description	Cash in	Cash out	Balance
Total				

Date:

Signed:

Daily Cash Flow Log Book

Date: From To

Prev. Balance:

Date	Description	Cash in	Cash out	Balance
Total				

Date:

Signed:

Daily Cash Flow Log Book

Date: From To

Prev. Balance:

Date	Description	Cash in	Cash out	Balance
Total				

Date:

Signed:

Daily Cash Flow Log Book

Date: From To

Prev. Balance:

Date	Description	Cash in	Cash out	Balance
Total				

Date:

Signed:

Daily Cash Flow Log Book

Date: From To

Prev. Balance:

Date	Description	Cash In	Cash Out	Balance
Total				

Date:

Signed:

Daily Cash Flow Log Book

Date: From To

Prev. Balance:

Date	Description	Cash in	Cash out	Balance
Total				

Date:

Signed:

Daily Cash Flow Log Book

Date: From To

Prev. Balance:

Date	Description	Cash in	Cash out	Balance
Total				

Date:

Signed:

Daily Cash Flow Log Book

Date: From To

Prey. Balance:

Date	Description	Cash in	Cash out	Balance
Total				

Date:

Signed:

Daily Cash Flow Log Book

Date: From To

Prev. Balance:

Date	Description	Cash in	Cash out	Balance
Total				

Date:

Signed:

Daily Cash Flow Log Book

Date: From To

Prev. Balance:

Date	Description	Cash in	Cash out	Balance
Total				

Date:

Signed:

Daily Cash Flow Log Book

Date: From To

Prey. Balance:

Date	Description	Cash in	Cash out	Balance
	Total			

Date:

Signed:

Daily Cash Flow Log Book

Date: From To

Prev. Balance:

Date	Description	Cash in	Cash out	Balance
Total				

Date:

Signed:

Daily Cash Flow Log Book

Date: From To

Prey. Balance:

Date	Description	Cash in	Cash out	Balance
Total				

Date:

Signed:

Daily Cash Flow Log Book

Date: From To

Prev. Balance:

Date	Description	Cash in	Cash out	Balance
Total				

Date:

Signed:

Daily Cash Flow Log Book

Date: From To

Prev. Balance:

Date	Description	Cash in	Cash out	Balance
Total				

Date:

Signed:

Daily Cash Flow Log Book

Date: From To

Prev. Balance:

Date	Description	Cash in	Cash out	Balance
Total				

Date:

Signed:

Daily Cash Flow Log Book

Date: From To

Prey. Balance:

Date	Description	Cash in	Cash out	Balance
Total				

Date:

Signed:

Daily Cash Flow Log Book

Date: From To

Prey. Balance:

Date	Description	Cash in	Cash out	Balance
Total				

Date:

Signed:

Daily Cash Flow Log Book

Date: From To

Prev. Balance:

Date	Description	Cash in	Cash out	Balance
Total				

Date:

Signed:

Daily Cash Flow Log Book

Date: From To

Prev. Balance:

Date	Description	Cash in	Cash out	Balance
Total				

Date:

Signed:

Daily Cash Flow Log Book

Date: From To

Prev. Balance:

Date	Description	Cash in	Cash out	Balance
Total				

Date:

Signed:

Daily Cash Flow Log Book

Date: From To

Prey. Balance:

Date	Description	Cash In	Cash Out	Balance
Total				

Date:

Signed:

Daily Cash Flow Log Book

Date: From To

Prev. Balance:

Date	Description	Cash in	Cash out	Balance
Total				

Date:

Signed:

Daily Cash Flow Log Book

Date: From   To

Prey. Balance:

Date	Description	Cash in	Cash out	Balance
Total				

Date:

Signed:

Daily Cash Flow Log Book

Date: From To

Prev. Balance:

Date	Description	Cash in	Cash out	Balance
Total				

Date:

Signed:

Daily Cash Flow Log Book

Date: From To

Prey. Balance:

Date	Description	Cash In	Cash Out	Balance
Total				

Date:

Signed:

Daily Cash Flow Log Book

Date: From To

Prev. Balance:

Date	Description	Cash in	Cash out	Balance
Total				

Date:

Signed:

Daily Cash Flow Log Book

Date: From To

Prev. Balance:

Date	Description	Cash in	Cash out	Balance
Total				

Date:

Signed:

Daily Cash Flow Log Book

Date: From To

Prev. Balance:

Date	Description	Cash in	Cash out	Balance
Total				

Date:

Signed:

Daily Cash Flow Log Book

Date: From To

Prev. Balance:

Date	Description	Cash In	Cash Out	Balance
Total				

Date:

Signed:

Daily Cash Flow Log Book

Date: From To

Prev. Balance:

Date	Description	Cash in	Cash out	Balance
Total				

Date:

Signed:

DAILY CASH FLOW LOG BOOK

DATE: FROM TO

PREV. BALANCE:

DATE	DESCRIPTION	CASH IN	CASH OUT	BALANCE
TOTAL				

DATE:

SIGNED:

Daily Cash Flow Log Book

Date: From To

Prey. Balance:

Date	Description	Cash in	Cash out	Balance
Total				

Date:

Signed:

Daily Cash Flow Log Book

Date: From To

Prev. Balance:

Date	Description	Cash in	Cash out	Balance
Total				

Date:

Signed:

Daily Cash Flow Log Book

Date: From To

Prev. Balance:

Date	Description	Cash in	Cash out	Balance
Total				

Date:

Signed:

Daily Cash Flow Log Book

Date: From To

Prey. Balance:

Date	Description	Cash in	Cash out	Balance
Total				

Date:

Signed:

Daily Cash Flow Log Book

Date: From To

Prev. Balance:

Date	Description	Cash in	Cash out	Balance
Total				

Date:

Signed:

Daily Cash Flow Log Book

Date: From To

Prey. Balance:

Date	Description	Cash in	Cash out	Balance
Total				

Date:

Signed:

Daily Cash Flow Log Book

Date: From To

Prev. Balance:

Date	Description	Cash in	Cash out	Balance
Total				

Date:

Signed:

Daily Cash Flow Log Book

Date: From To

Prev. Balance:

Date	Description	Cash In	Cash Out	Balance
Total				

Date:

Signed:

Daily Cash Flow Log Book

Date: From To

Prev. Balance:

Date	Description	Cash in	Cash out	Balance
Total				

Date:

Signed:

Daily Cash Flow Log Book

Date: From To

Prey. Balance:

Date	Description	Cash in	Cash out	Balance
Total				

Date:

Signed:

Daily Cash Flow Log Book

Date: From To

Prev. Balance:

Date	Description	Cash in	Cash out	Balance
Total				

Date:

Signed:

DAILY CASH FLOW LOG BOOK

DATE: FROM TO

PREV. BALANCE:

DATE	DESCRIPTION	CASH IN	CASH OUT	BALANCE
TOTAL				

DATE:

SIGNED:

Daily Cash Flow Log Book

Date: From To

Prev. Balance:

Date	Description	Cash in	Cash out	Balance
Total				

Date:

Signed:

Daily Cash Flow Log Book

Date: From To

Prev. Balance:

Date	Description	Cash In	Cash Out	Balance
Total				

Date:

Signed:

Daily Cash Flow Log Book

Date: From To

Prev. Balance:

Date	Description	Cash in	Cash out	Balance
Total				

Date:

Signed:

Daily Cash Flow Log Book

Date: From To

Prev. Balance:

Date	Description	Cash in	Cash out	Balance
Total				

Date:

Signed:

DAILY CASH FLOW LOG BOOK

DATE: FROM TO

PREV. BALANCE:

DATE	DESCRIPTION	CASH IN	CASH OUT	BALANCE
TOTAL				

DATE:

SIGNED:

Daily Cash Flow Log Book

Date: From To

Prey. Balance:

Date	Description	Cash in	Cash out	Balance
Total				

Date:

Signed:

Daily Cash Flow Log Book

Date: From To

Prev. Balance:

Date	Description	Cash in	Cash out	Balance
Total				

Date:

Signed:

Daily Cash Flow Log Book

Date: From To

Prey. Balance:

Date	Description	Cash in	Cash out	Balance
Total				

Date:

Signed:

Daily Cash Flow Log Book

Date: From To

Prev. Balance:

Date	Description	Cash in	Cash out	Balance
Total				

Date:

Signed:

DAILY CASH FLOW LOG BOOK

DATE: FROM TO

PREV. BALANCE:

DATE	DESCRIPTION	CASH IN	CASH OUT	BALANCE
TOTAL				

DATE:

SIGNED:

Daily Cash Flow Log Book

Date: From To

Prey. Balance:

Date	Description	Cash in	Cash out	Balance
Total				

Date:

Signed:

Daily Cash Flow Log Book

Date: From To

Prev. Balance:

Date	Description	Cash in	Cash out	Balance
Total				

Date:

Signed:

Daily Cash Flow Log Book

Date: From To

Prev. Balance:

Date	Description	Cash in	Cash out	Balance
Total				

Date:

Signed:

Daily Cash Flow Log Book

Date: From To

Prev. Balance:

Date	Description	Cash in	Cash out	Balance
Total				

Date:

Signed:

Daily Cash Flow Log Book

Date: From To

Prev. Balance:

Date	Description	Cash in	Cash out	Balance
Total				

Date:

Signed:

Daily Cash Flow Log Book

Date: From To

Prev. Balance:

Date	Description	Cash in	Cash out	Balance
Total				

Date:

Signed:

Daily Cash Flow Log Book

Date: From To

Prev. Balance:

Date	Description	Cash in	Cash out	Balance
Total				

Date:

Signed:

Daily Cash Flow Log Book

Date: From To

Prey. Balance:

Date	Description	Cash in	Cash out	Balance
Total				

Date:

Signed:

Daily Cash Flow Log Book

Date: From To

Prev. Balance:

Date	Description	Cash in	Cash out	Balance
Total				

Date:

Signed:

DAILY CASH FLOW LOG BOOK

DATE: FROM To

PREY. BALANCE:

DATE	DESCRIPTION	CASH IN	CASH OUT	BALANCE
TOTAL				

DATE:

SIGNED:

DAILY CASH FLOW LOG BOOK

DATE: FROM TO

PREV. BALANCE:

DATE	DESCRIPTION	CASH IN	CASH OUT	BALANCE
TOTAL				

DATE:

SIGNED:

Daily Cash Flow Log Book

Date: From To

Prey. Balance:

Date	Description	Cash in	Cash out	Balance
Total				

Date:

Signed:

Daily Cash Flow Log Book

Date: From To

Prey. Balance:

Date	Description	Cash in	Cash out	Balance
Total				

Date:

Signed:

Daily Cash Flow Log Book

Date: From To

Prev. Balance:

Date	Description	Cash in	Cash out	Balance
Total				

Date:

Signed:

Hello

Thank you so much for purchasing our book.

Please rate the book with the stars it deserves and write your opinion, your review helps us improve our quality.

Thank you very much!

Made in the USA
Monee, IL
19 January 2022

89369482R00061